# Thinker's Journey

By

## *Hod*

*Fifth Edition*

© 2004-5 Hod Doering
All rights reserved

Published by

The Poetry Barn
1634 North Elliston-Trowbridge Road
Graytown, Ohio
USA
43432

# Table of contents

The Thinking Highway .................................................................. 1
Terminology ................................................................................. 2
Planning our trip - Why this book ................................................. 4
To Think Or Not To Think? Isn't that the question? ...................... 6
Rules of the Road: Thinking Basic Rules and Tools ..................... 9
    Making Connections ............................................................... 9
    Basic Definitions .................................................................... 13
    Problem Types ....................................................................... 17
    The Scientific Method ............................................................ 23
    Creating Smaller Problems .................................................... 25
    Same But Different ................................................................ 26
    PST General Rule 5 .............................................................. 28
Rules for breaking rules ............................................................. 33
    Brainstorming Ground Rules ................................................ 34
    Brainstorming Steps ............................................................. 36
The Best Places to see: Creative Thinking ............................... 39
    You can be a creative thinker ............................................... 39
    Cultivating Inspiration, Intuition and insight .......................... 40
    Turn Off Your Editor ............................................................. 42
    What to do when you don't know what to do ....................... 46
    Insight .................................................................................. 47
    Consider Go-ghoti – Language Puzzler ............................... 55
Drive This Way: The Art of Thinking ......................................... 57
Future Journeys: Discipline-Specific Thinking Tools ................. 62
    Specialized thinking ............................................................. 62
    Mathematical Thinking ......................................................... 65
    Scientific Thinking ................................................................ 66
    Philosophical Thinking: Formal Logic ................................. 66
    Computer Programming Thinking ....................................... 67
    Engineering Thinking ........................................................... 68
    Art & Creative Thinking ........................................................ 68
After-word .................................................................................. 70
Appendix A: Creating Your Thinking Toolbox ........................... 71
Appendix B: Thinking Styles ..................................................... 74
Appendix C: Suggested Pedagogy ........................................... 75
Appendix D: More Thinking Road Signs & Roadside Attractions.... 77
Appendix E: List of PST Rules ................................................. 80
    Creative Thinking Rules ...................................................... 80
    General Thinking Rules ...................................................... 80
Glossary of Important Terms ..................................................... 81
Further Resources ..................................................................... 86
Index .......................................................................................... 89

# The Thinking Highway

Lao Tzu said "A journey of a thousand miles begins with a single step." Often we ask if the journey is worth the traveling. Sometimes we ask what is that first step. For your thinking journey this text is a way to take that first step.

There is no attempt in this text to get anyone to think like a genius or to become a world class thinker although there is nothing to prevent that either. Rather the goal of this book is to provide a firm foundation for educators and students alike to build problem solving thinking upon, both in a general sense and as an introduction to discipline-specific thinking styles in future courses.

In order to promote awareness of future uses and styles of thought some introduction is provided in the final section, Discipline-Specific Thinking Tools with more referenced in appendix B. This book is meant to connect skills learned here to other courses and disciplines. There is no attempt to be exhaustive in either presentation or explanation of discipline-specific thinking skills.

The bibliography contains references, books and websites, to further enhance thinking skills and provide practice.

# Terminology

The metaphor of a road trip as a reflection of the thinking journey is loosely carried through the sections using these basic ideas:

<u>Words You Need To Know</u> will be underlined and can be found in the Glossary. Make a list of these terms as you go along. This is a major part of your <u>PST Toolbox</u>. See Appendix A: Creating Your Thinking Toolbox, to begin.

A <u>Scenic Overlook</u> provides a higher level perspective or a summary of points.

A <u>Side Trip</u> is listed as such to indicate that it is an illustrative and pleasurable junket away from the main thrust of the text (highway) to highlights or related ideas that support rather directly the main text. Do not skip these journeys.

A <u>Bustling Backwater</u> is information and sometimes exercises that can expand the thinking experience. These are the equivalent of a wilderness hiker turning into a canyon not on her map and seeing a small herd of wild horses or that of turning down a previously untraveled back road a few miles from your home to find a functioning cider mill. Although these may be skipped without damage to the basic goal of the text they are designed to provide enrichment and further depth to the thinking experiences herein.

A <u>Road</u> <u>Sign</u> is a short statement or idea that may be relevant and provide some cause for discussion and thought, but often is not pursued directly, at least in the section where it appears. Some refer back to previous sections. Others foreshadow coming text.

The term <u>Roadside</u> <u>Attraction</u> is used to indicate areas where students can practice using their thinking skills on the ideas that are presented or those that they develop. In a traditional text these might be called exercises. In responding to these it is suggested that students be given wide latitude in the manner of their responses whenever possible to promote varied approach skills as well as to allow for different learning styles and background interests.

The term <u>PPP</u>, an acronym for Page, Poem or Picture is used as a shorthand for this generic response idea, but the response alternatives are limited only by your imagination. Write a short play or song. Create your own Road Sign or Roadside Attraction.

The truth of the matter is that thinking is indeed a journey. Most thinkers would agree that their life journey is different than it would be without critical thinking skills and the abilities they provide to help appreciate the journey and to help solve its problems. The plan and hope for this text is that your critical and creative thinking journey begins here. Enjoy this journey and may it lead to lifelong enjoyment of thinking.

## Planning our trip - Why this book?

Why another thinking book? Thinking is a niche market that already has dozens if not hundreds of texts; so why another one? Current books are written for people who want to think about thinking or for those who wish to practice and hone existing thinking skills.

> Side Trip: Allow me to recall a day at the running track several decades ago. After working out for several weeks on the college indoor track it was a Check-day for me. A Check-day is a workout where you go for maximum effort to compare with previous times to show how much you have progressed. For me at this time my check was a two-lap sprint, 220 yards.
>
> I was running a good ten seconds ahead of my previous best time. I was sprinting at my best pace. I felt good. Breathing hard, but fully. I suddenly realized that I had been passed for the third time by these two joggers who weren't even breaking a sweat. They were chatting in a normal conversational tone as they loped past. I stumbled as I lost concentration. I almost fell on my face. My time was about fifteen seconds off my best as I limped across the line.
>
> I later found out that these two guys were top marathoners in Northwest Ohio. One of them was asked to try out for the American Olympic team. He had placed in the top ten or so in the Boston Marathon for the last several years.
>
> Recalling this incident I cannot help but wonder if many students have similar classroom stories. Do you have an incident in your classroom history when someone shut you down, mentally speaking, lapped you or made you look and feel ridiculous? Ever participate in a spelling bee? Many school and classroom exercises allow the Olympic thinkers to shine and leave little room for regular folks.

This book is written for new or apprentice thinkers as a foundation to thinking in their chosen profession or discipline. It can also be used as introduction to those books already out there.

People learn and think in many different ways. A primary goal of this book is to provide a common experience and vocabulary so that we can talk about, exercise and enhance thinking skills both in and out of the classroom.

This book is not meant to disallow the existence or validity of any other ideals or methodologies, rather it is trying to provide common foundation for thinking both in the individual and, consequently, in the educational or training process. This book assumes thinking can be taught and practiced like math, writing or running.

Its goal is to provide the reader with a basic toolbox of thinking skills and a vocabulary of thinking and talking about thinking.

---

### Roadside Attraction 01

PPP us sharing your worst moment in thinking. Never made any mistakes? Maybe you're just not trying hard enough. Perhaps a PPP detailing a thinking or problem solving victory is in order?

## To Think Or Not To Think?
### Isn't that the question?

Is there any question as to whether or not we should think? If we ask a different question: Do we think we should think more or better? Or how can I think better? Is the overall answer any easier? Many people seem to avoid thinking as much as possible, allowing others to decide for them. If you choose not to decide you have made a choice. Although it may be easier in the short run to allow others to do our thinking for us there is almost always a cost in the long run. There has been a major block to the teaching of thinking in the past. It was assumed by many that some folks could think better or more logically or different because they were somehow wired that way. Traditionally, many instructors thought that you could no

> Bazooka Joe on a Bazooka bubble gum cartoon from the fifties:
> A fool and his money are soon partied!

> Side Trip: Consider the idea of teaching tall. You can teach/train someone to safely use a ladder or stepstool, tools to extend reach.
>
> You can teach and train someone to jump higher. Do you recall the five-six professional basketball player who won a slam-dunk contest against seven-footers a few years ago? Spudd Webb?

> ### Roadside Attraction 00
> Think of reasons why *THINK* may be considered a 4-letter word. Give reasons why *LOVE* is not a 4-letter word.
>
> One goal of this book is to learn how to handle this type of problem. We'll visit this one again later.

more teach thinking than you could teach tall. People either are thinkers or they are not; thinking even seemed to run in families like height.

In the past, most college faculty seemed to believe that, at best, "You can lead students to knowledge, but you cannot make them think!" Since no amount of teaching would help those who could not get it why try. This has led many students to regard think as just another 4-letter word.

Research and practice has shown that people can become better thinkers if they work on it, talk about it and practice it, just like reading, math, history, composition, basketball, baseball or computer programming. I agree with this point of view and it is assumed in this book that thinking can indeed be taught and that you, the student, can get better at it by learning its specific vocabulary, concepts and techniques. I can only hope that your experience herein further supports this.

Why think? (It should be obvious to you by now on which side of the original question my loyalties place me.) A more specific question is why should you bother to learn to think better or more fully?

You will need to provide this answer for yourself, but here are my . . .

Top Eight Reasons I Think:

8) It is fun to be able to solve problems and to share the process with a team of capable problem solvers.

7) You'll always be quick enough with the best comeback when your friends slam you.

6) You perform better in any game, class or situation if your mind is better trained, just as a better trained athlete wins more often.

5) Since many people do not think well your skills mean you will be more effective and more $valued$.

4) Every moment of every day looks different when consciously considered; one actually feels more alive.

3) You are more in control of your life when you can think and solve problems effectively.

2) Everyone nods and smiles at your deep wisdom.

1) You can never be bored when you have access to the trillion billion universes inside a working mind.

## Rules of the Road
Thinking Basic Rules and Tools

This book plans to lead you safely down that often bumpy highway to careful, random and crazy thinking. Crazy, I hear you say! I have spent a lifetime trying to be considered normal and now you want to drive me crazy?!? Welcome to the sometimes rocky, but often rewarding and always interesting world of thought. By the way for most of us it is not a drive to crazy rather a short chip and a putt, to use a golfing reference mixed in with a rather cross-wise <u>pun</u> so don't be so surprised that some of what you have nearly perfected to this point may need to be modified or even completely discarded as we acquire new skills and ideas.

Making Connections

People who think seriously often enjoy puns, not so much for their humor as for their echoes in the mind. Puns, when at all successful, make the hearer work and cause connections that may never have been connected before. While many of those actual connections could be quite trivial the process of making those connections and their eventual uses give a major start toward Problem Solving Thinking and eventually, by a semi-amazing side journey coincidence, to those clear clean mountain streams of <u>Critical Thinking</u> and the marvelous cloud canyons of <u>Creative Thinking</u>.

> **Roadside Attraction 02**
>
> But enough about me. Is it odd yet? Are you feeling challenged? Well here's a challenge: Create a pun, no create twenty-one puns, create a twenty-one pun salute to your learning to this point and the acquisition of this new Thinking Tool. For more examples ask those around you to share theirs. If you simply cannot manage twenty-one puns on your own in the time allotted perhaps you could make two friends and create seven puns each or could you allow yourself to make six friends and do three each. Is that <u>Cheating</u> or is it creative problem solving?

While you're working I'll share one of my favorite puns that I heard from my daughter when she was in the sixth grade. To have it work properly it needs to be said out loud, not written, but I think the loss of surprise to you now may be justified by the larger gain of an entire class of humor and its associated <u>Thinking</u> <u>Tools</u>. Person the puns: "What does a fish say when it hits a concrete wall?" The answer: "Dam!"

I know you got the humor, but did it help you to create your twenty-one puns? Perhaps a bit of explanation, a good pun, as I believe this is, must work on more than one level. It is the echoes of the arcing of the connections crashing together in your mind more than the actual humor of the saying. We juxtapose the sleepy image of the

> Bustling Backwater: My fish was a rainbow trout. What type of fish was yours? My fish's name was Abnergonia; he was two years old and originally hailed from northern Ontario.

swimming fish with the literally concrete image of man's intrusion. Of course that is much less than humorous. The humor of this pun comes from the double meaning of the sound of the word "Dam" with the word "Damn," one of those naughty words on that long list of words you once wished you might find in the dictionary. This is exactly the type of grade school humor which most of us pretend we have left behind in our journeys thus far. Another delight for most is the rediscovery of the fact that, indeed, we do still have positive connections of and to our youth.

Another favorite joke of mine uses a sort of reverse punning. The Story: It seems an Englishman came to tour America in the late-middle thirties to see for himself this whole Great Depression Thing which was making all the news in Europe. He traveled across the Midwest noting with some consternation that farms still seemed to be growing plenty of food while people in cities starved. Farms were in danger of going under because they were unable to sell their fresh produce.

One Ohio Corn Farmer summed up the attitude in a rhyming pun, typical of Midwest make-do philosophy and wit. "Well we eat what corn we can, and what we can't eat we can!" The English visitor was delighted and determined then and there to share this wisdom and wit with his fellows back at his local pub.

In due time that moment came. He had finished his erudite overview and evaluation of The American Situation and paused for effect and attention. "It seems," he orated, "That those hardy American Farmers have a catchphrase to sum it all up.  They say they eat what corn they can and what they cannot eat . . . (pause for mental drum roll)  . . . they put up in tins!"  I find English-persons seem to find this more uproarious than Americans in this current century, but I put this down to the fact that most Americans nowadays are not aware that can has never been a transitive verb in England and could probably not care less.

While good puns do make subtle connections for you, so what?  Well, in thinking about and through things, in solving any real problems you often need to make similarly tenuous and new cross-connections for yourself.  Almost all true problems have some small or large amount of necessary information missing; in some cases the information doesn't even exist and must be created.  If all the information was obviously there it would probably not be much of a problem, perhaps barely an exercise.  This is where your PST ToolBox, carefully organized and packed with all your Thinking Tools, can come in handy.

---

### Scenic Overlook

Another term native to this book is PST, which stands for Problem Solving Thinking.  Think of a little helper person who keeps these rules and terms straight for you whispering PSsssssT in your ear whenever help is needed.

## Basic Definitions

<u>Problem</u> & <u>Exercise</u>.  If we already know how to solve a question, situation or puzzle completely then it is not a Problem, rather it is an Exercise.  Questions or situations which should be exercises (or are exercises for some) become problems if we do not have the appropriate skills or the ability to correctly apply them.  This is why most students need to learn specific thinking skills and need practice applying them in order to consistently succeed.  Just like a runner gets better with practice running, the more you think the better you get.

I can recall many students over the last 30 years stating something like, "It's pretty easy once you get it."  This booklet is designed to lay a foundation for students to get it and for instructors to help them get it in basic and in more advanced applications.

Let's examine our basic vehicle by looking at some Stages of Comprehension in human learning.  You need to have a set of rules for problems that are the same as ones you have encountered before.

> Side Trip:  Sometimes the thought doesn't need to be that deep or that long.  It is an excellent skill to know when to think deeply and when to go with the obvious.  Are we agreed that 2+2 is an example of the latter?  We might call this a No-Brainer in the vernacular of the last century.

Arithmetic contains a set of these rules or algorithms. If you need to know the sum of two numbers you use the addition rules. For most of us those rules have been practiced beyond the point of rules and into the Zone of <u>Unconscious</u> <u>Comprehension</u>. The subtraction rules work that way for most of us as well. How about the addition or subtraction of negative numbers, long division, Lowest Common Denominator and division of fractions. Are these examples of arithmetic rules that have or have not made it into your Zone of Unconscious Comprehension, or do they remain in your Zone of <u>Conscious</u> <u>Comprehension</u> or are they currently languishing in that vast Zone of <u>Incomprehension</u>.

One example of a <u>human</u> <u>learning</u> <u>rule</u> is the <u>3000</u> <u>times</u> <u>rule</u> which states that it takes approximately 3000 repetitions for an idea, action, rule or deed to become automatic and natural. A <u>corollary</u> might be the statement, "The harder I work, the luckier I get, " a paraphrase of a quote attributed to both Benjamin Franklin and Thomas Jefferson. Or the proverb, "Practice makes perfect."

> ### Scenic Overlook
> This means that you should have to think about thinking in new channels or manners for quite a while before it becomes natural. Surprise!

---

### Roadside Attraction 03

Do you agree that the more you practice the better you get? Are there limitations or exceptions to this rule? Any corollaries or broader applications you can think of? Write one page listing and considering these three questions and the repetition or practice theory from your point of view.

---

If you are learning something for class you need to go through it, work it or read it a minimum of three times to be familiar with it. Somewhere around 300 times through you achieve Conscious Comprehension, but it is not until you have used it successfully 3000 times that you make it seem natural, also called Unconscious Comprehension or so said an old karate instructor of mine.

How many times have you done addition problems? Subtraction? Long division? How about fractions and percent problems?

Sit-ups? Laps around the track? How often have you thought lately about those things you never think about . . . but do regularly?

For people who are good at word problems the problem solving process has become automatic; they have passed their 3000 times point and the process, in many cases the actual information, has become natural or automatically available. For most of us this would be the equivalent exercise level of "2 + 2 = 4."

> **Roadside Attraction 04**
>
> Write down ten things you do most every day that you never need to stop and think about. Can you also list ten things you did in the past week that you had to spend time thinking about?

How about those things you don't know. Do you think you know everything there is to know? If you know everything then you can learn nothing.

Socratic wisdom: The beginning of knowledge is the acceptance of ignorance.

> Student: "I know everything"  Master: "Then you know nothing."
> Student: "I know nothing."  Master: "Now you can begin to learn everything."

We seldom dwell on how little we know. The more I learn the more I realize how little I truly know.

> Once you can see over the mountain you can see the real mountains beyond

> BUSTLING BACKWATER: Did you know there was an Encyclopedia of Ignorance published in 1979 listing the opinions of many of the world's great physical scientists and thinkers on what we are truly ignorant about. It is an interesting read.

### Roadside Attraction 05

List fifteen things you are sure you do not know. Share your ignorance. Go online and search a bookseller to see how many books have the word Ignorance in their title. Ask yourself and each other how many of those things you would really like to know. Are any of them important enough to work toward learning? Compile a class list to share with other sections or terms.

Bustling Backwater: Many students consciously avoid career choices because of the thinking required. I recall a student from the mid-seventies who had an opposite problem. He was having problems in my remedial math class. In his frustration one day he shouted out in class, "I don't want to learn this ?<?#$@ math, I just want to be an engineer!!"

Although somewhat disruptive this was a breakthrough for this student. When we took the time to talk to the engineering faculty and let this student look at some engineering textbooks he saw how much of engineering was math and logical thinking using math; he began to actually work at learning the math foundations we were teaching and was much more successful.

## Problem Types

There are three basic divisions we should make here in the type or category of problem that needs us to supply missing information or take some new action.

General Problem Type 1, the Old Problem (See Exercise.) is that class of problem that we have seen before, perhaps solved successfully many times. The missing information in the problem is well known to us and we probably need to do little or no Conscious Thinking to get the information and the desired answer.

Problem Angle 1: let us consider one problem many of us would put into this Old class, finding the area of a rectangular room for wall-to-wall carpeting. We

> Bustling Backwater: Rule Of Life 1702: You can get almost anything to fit almost anywhere if you push hard enough or cut it up small enough. Corollary 1: Sometimes both. Corollary 2: This doesn't guarantee you'll like the way it looks when you're done.

simply measure the length and then the width of the room. Multiplication or a calculator gives us the area. If you've ever laid carpeting you know that you actually need to add some carpet at each side and end to cut off when you put it down, but the basic measuring and area problem is an Old Problem.

Problem Angle 2: Consider the same basic problem from a different angle. What if we have a room with a 42 foot perimeter and want to put a 10 foot by 10 foot area rug into it without cutting the rug.

If we can measure one wall, let's say it measures 10.2 feet, then we can calculate the other wall from the known perimeter value of 42 feet at 10.8 feet and say yes, the rug will fit nicely. What does it do for the answer if the wall we measure is 9.2 feet instead? How about 11 feet? 12 feet?

Problem Angle 3: What if you needed to carpet a wall? Paint a wall? Carpet the ceiling? How about hanging a large painting?

Have all these problem situations happened before in your life? Did you always solve them yourself? Do all of these problems seem roughly the same to you? Did you classify all three of these angles as Old Problems for you? Did you solve them easily and quickly with (or without) pencil and paper? Was your answer to any of these questions "NO?"

Let us consider the solution of Problem Angle 1 in more detail. Got your Question Bag packed? Thinking ToolBox strapped tightly? Yes!

> Bustling Backwater: Have you ever noticed that "NO" is "ON" backwards? And upside down? If you stand on your head and look at an "ON" light switch it says "NO." If it says "ON" when you are upside down then it is installed upside down and your light is turning on backwards. Has it complained? Does it seem distressed? Does the light coming out look any different? NO? Then why do they have those little labels on there if it doesn't make any difference? Do you know any electrical engineers or physicists? Ask one. You might enjoy the look on their face if not the actual answer or lack of one. Do you think an electrician might give you a different answer? Make a guess then rent or borrow one to find out.

Let's see if there is indeed a similarity between these problem angles. The number one question which I am sure you each have in your Question Bag even if otherwise empty is, "Where do we start?" In other words, "Where do you start if you don't know where to start?" It helps to have a ToolBox with some rules in it as well as definitions and concepts.

The first rule you will put into your Thinking Toolbox is one that can

> "The Facts, Maam, just the Facts," as Joe Friday used to say on fifties TV.

start us off on almost any problem because it is simply three questions. Let's call it <u>PST General Rule One</u>. Like most of the PST rules we shall encounter herein
this rule has two components, questions and steps. The first Question is, "What information has the problem given us?"

Why don't we write this out as a list under the heading, Given (Fig 1). It should look something like this for that first problem:

Fig 1:
GIVEN
A.  We want to lay down some carpet wall-to-wall
B.  Our room is rectangular
C.  Finding the area of the room will give us the answer

Now we want to see what else we have stored in our mind or its immediate vicinity that could possibly relate to this problem. Why don't we write this out as a list under the heading Known beside the heading Given (Fig 2). It should look something like this for that first problem:

Fig 2:

| GIVEN | KNOWN |
|---|---|
| A. We want to lay down some carpet wall-to-wall | A. Call carpet store for install and measuring info wall-to-wall |
| B. Our room is rectangular | B. opposite walls of rectangle are equal length |
| C. Finding the area of the room will give us the answer | C. A = L x W |
|  | D. How to use a tape measure |

We might have thrown in that our cousin's fiancée installs carpet so we could invite them over for breakfast Saturday and . . . hmm. But that would be <u>Cheating</u>.

You will often have many more choices of things you know that could relate or many more people you could call. The trick is to decide which ones work for a given problem. You will get better at this trick the more you use you thinking skills.

---

**Roadside Attraction 06**

Apply PSTGR1 for yourself to the other questions in Problem Angles 2 & 3. It may take a few minutes so you should get pencil and paper as well as an appropriate refreshment suite. Go ahead. I'll wait.

Well, did it work pretty well? Compare your application and experience using PSTGR1 to that of a friend or classmate. You may wish to write a paragraph or five detailing and comparing both.

Why don't we write this out as a list under the heading Need beside the heading Known (Fig 3).

It should look something like this for that first problem:

Fig 3:

| GIVEN | KNOWN | NEED |
|---|---|---|
| A. We want to lay down some carpet wall-to-wall | A. Call carpet store for install and measuring info wall-to-wall | A. extra carpet needed on all sides to install wall-to-wall |
| B. Our room is rectangular | B. opposite walls of rectangle are equal length | B. Measure two adjacent walls |
| C. Finding the area of the room will give us the answer | C. A = L x W | C. Calculate answer Convert to square yards because carpet is sold by square yards not square feet |
|  | D. How to use a tape measure | D. Measure wall end-to-end NOT top to bottom |

As we have looked up, imagined or otherwise gotten information we may add it to our Known column and add other items to our Need column. In a changing problem situation items may even be added to our Given column.

The nice thing about <u>PST General Rule 1</u> (PSTGR1) is that it can be generally applied in very much this same manner to almost every problem. The larger and more complex the problem or question the more steps and items you may have, but processes (rules) are similar. General Problem Type 2, the <u>New Problem</u>, is that class of problem where you have never seen it or anything like it; maybe you have never even thought about the concepts involved. Not only is some information missing, but so are some or even all of the basic concepts.

One example of this type would be the idea of human teleportation from Earth to Mars. You might have encountered the basic idea in a book or on a TV program, but it is unlikely that you have solved the practical problem before or you would be off collecting your Nobel Prize instead of reading this book. Consider this problem from a practical view point for a moment. We cannot hope to solve the problem here, but maybe we can use our tools to attack it, to break it down into its parts.

> ### Roadside Attraction 07
>
> Use PSTGR1 for this teleportation problem and share your solution with classmates. Are we famous yet? Rich? Do we need some more thinking tools? For now let us get on with our problem types and then to more tools.

General Problem Type 3, the <u>Mixed Problem</u>, is that class of problem we most often encounter where some of it is new, but some of it is rather familiar, at least after we break the problem down using our tools. We personally may have not solved much of it, but someone has. Almost all schoolroom problems fall into this problem type. So do many, though not all, business and practical problems. Most problems, those things needing solution rather

than only exercise, seem to fall into this type and require Combined Solution, a little bit of creativity and a lot of elbow grease and footwork.  This is our One-Three Punch.
In order to solve as many as possible of this type we will need a more complete toolbox and some practice with our tools.  More about this problem type later.

## The Scientific Method

Let us consider a tool that may be new to many thinkers called <u>The Scientific Method.</u>  This is a tried and true method of problem solving which leads to a whole set of thinking and Problem Solving Thinking skills.  The basic idea is simple.  Make a guess or an observation then prove or disprove it by experiment.  To formalize the process they use the term <u>Hypothesis</u> for the guess or observation you wish to support.  Then we gather data, relevant information, by study, observation or experiment.  This type of data is called Empirical Data and is only trusted if it can be repeated by others with essentially the same result.  Not all Hypotheses can be tested this way.  Some can only be subjected to thought such as our idea of transmitting human beings over great distances as if they were a television signal.  For these we have the concept of the <u>Thought Experiment</u>.  A thought experiment can be tested by others, which means they go through your same ideas in the same order to reach similar conclusions.  As you might guess there are many more disagreements over thought experiments than physical experiments.

Let us take one simple example: Is there Gravity in your house? State your Hypothesis.

> **Roadside Attraction 08**
> Use the Scientific Method to prove that wind exists. PPP your conclusions.

There is Gravity in my house. How do you prove Gravity? What is Gravity? How does it manifest itself? Can I hear it? Can I see it? Can I measure it?

Notice the larger question mandates that we ask smaller ones first. Does this look a lot like PSTGR1? What is Given? What do we know? What do we Need? In this case the only given is The Scientific Method: Hypothesis, Test, Conclusion. Let us call The Scientific Method our <u>PST</u> <u>General</u> <u>Rule</u> <u>2</u>.

Now to our problem. Do we know what Gravity is? Can we gain a significant majority of our peers to agree that Gravity means when you let go of a glass of water in mid-air the glass falls down to whatever surface lies below it? I would wager that we can gain that agreement. So all we need to do is to let go of the glass full of water in the air over our kitchen floor and see if there is Gravity at home. Try it.

Did you all think to use a paper cup so that there would be no glass fallout? Did it work? Yes. Did it surprise anyone? I should hope not. We assume Gravity exists in our home at all times don't we?

Is anyone worried about falling up or floating away when they get up or go to bed?
If so, that is a different type of thinking called Crazy Thinking which is not bad on its own, but can become a problem if it becomes an obsession or if it completely overwhelms Regular Thinking.

## Creating Smaller Problems

Many problems are simply too big to solve in one chunk. So what do we do? Quit? Hire a better problem solver? Wait for somebody else to tell us what to do? All of these are valid answers, but none of these are the way thinkers approach big problems. Is it possible that there are several smaller problems which, if solved, lead to a solution for this Too Big Problem? If we can find those smaller problems by breaking down this Too Big Problem into smaller, easier problems then we can make our job a lot easier and get to a solution more easily. What if one of these smaller problems remains a Too Big Problem? Can we apply this creating smaller problems rule again to this new problem? Yes we can. We can continue to apply it as long as we can make the valid link that the smaller solutions will support the original. That is, proving all of the individual smaller problems really does prove the original Too Big Problem. Let's call this new rule of creating smaller, easier problems our PST General Rule 3.

## Same But Different

<u>Same</u> <u>and/but</u> <u>different</u>: When you break a problem into smaller pieces you need to break out any familiar parts, Old Problems. This often gives a partial solution. You need to be careful not to be fooled by problems that appear to be the same, but have different root causes. This is an addition to PSTGR1 since our Same category can be considered Known and our Different category could fall under the Need column. Make a PST Card as <u>PST</u> <u>General</u> <u>Rule</u> <u>4</u> and add a reference to it to PSTGR1's card.

When you look at a problem can you say it is just like one you have met before with exceptions? Are the exceptions

> Side Trip: In Northwestern Ohio, perhaps much of the Midwest, we use a fairly common saying or idea, "just the same, but different" to compare items. This phrase confused a colleague of mine who was originally from Canada. He asked me how something can be the same and also be different. He made me think. (I thank him very much for that.) The phrase is most often used something like, "My sister has a sweater just like that, but it's blue." where the sweater in reference is red or some other non-blue color, but has properties very much like this sweater. It is often misused by overstating the first case and having an unreasonable number of qualifications such as "My cousin dated a guy just like you, but he was taller and had short black hair instead of long blonde hair and he was an engineer instead of a dancer and he always wore a tie and I think he died or got married to another engineer type." This is sloppy sentence construction as well as muddy thinking. One gets the impression that the two dates in question probably only had their maleness in common.
>
> This concept can apply to problems as well. A simple example would be 2+2 which we mentioned earlier and agreed that 4 was our solution. If we now ask what is 3+5 can we agree this is just the same, but different? I use the same process with different numbers to get 8 as our answer.

large or small? Can you list the items that make it the same? List the items that make it different. Beware of two things in this process: 1) It is a tendency to want things to be familiar. This is much more comfortable. Therefore, after you create your lists double check that the items in your Same list really are things you have solved before and that they each apply appropriately to the current problem. 2) Make sure that items in your different list are not just variations of an Old Problem.

---

### Roadside Attraction 09

Did you know that there are different number systems? Our standard number system is base 10. If you were using base 6 arithmetic the answer to the 2+2 would still be 4, but the answer to 3+5 would be 12 in base 6. Write out ten simple one-digit addition problems and write down the answers in our "normal" base 10. Leave two columns beside the base 10 answer. In these columns write the answer in base 8 and in base 2. Do they look odd? Did you need more room to write solutions in base 8? How about base 2? (You may need to look up information on base arithmetic to successfully complete this challenge. Looking up stuff is fun, so enjoy.) Is your brain full yet? No, try writing down ten simple subtraction problems and working those in the same three bases.

# **PST General Rule 5**

Our primary tool for <u>Formal Problem Solving</u> is a set of steps which can be applied to almost every problem.  Let us call this <u>PST General Rule 5</u>.  PSTGR5 consists of 6 steps:

1      Make a <u>Formal Statement Of The Problem</u>.   This could involve using several of the Basic Rules to isolate and specify the exact problem.

A single symptom can indicate more than one problem.  In business or life we often find similar confusions.  "It doesn't work" or "it won't start" in reference to a car or other machine may certainly be problematic, but means next to nothing in moving you to a valid solution. "We're losing money!" is a similar statement in a business setting.

> Side Trip:  Consider the problem, "I walked out this morning to my car and noticed my feet were wet." What is my problem?
>
> Many of you would have "Wet feet" as your first answer.  Yes?  Well, consider this, is that a problem or is it a Symptom?  Why are my feet wet and how do I fix it?
>
> Let us look at several different problems all of which might yield that same wet-foot symptom:
>
> I forgot to put my shoes on and the dew or rain from yesterday wetted my poor toe-sies.
>
> My shoes have holes in their soles, a problem similar to #1 with possibly different solutions or parameters:  can I afford new soles or do I have another pair to put on?
>
> I live on a river which floods every spring.  Changing shoes is not a solution, hip boots may be.  To resolve it for the long term may be rather more drastic calling for intervention of government agencies or buying of boats.
>
> Do you see how the same symptoms can indicate more than one problem.

In computer programming courses we hear "My program won't run." on a regular basis. Although these may be true statements they are misleading and usually unhelpful since they refer to symptoms not a particular question which can be answered or a specific problem to be solved.

2      Analyze The Problem: Brainstorming is often part of this stage. Critical Thinking of all types could be used here as well as Creative Thinking tools.  The goal here is to dissect and rearrange the problem statement from step 1 into something that can be solved or at least attempted.  Do NOT try to create the solution at the same time.  If it happens, as it sometimes does, that the analysis leads directly to known solutions of some or all of the problem stated in step 1 feel safe in going ahead.  Be careful not to force any particular solution at this step.

3      Develop The Solution: Turn the results of step 2 into a workable solution.  This could involve any combination of steps or sub-solutions that is deemed necessary and desirable.

4      Create The Solution: Make each stage of the solutions designed in Step 3 happen. Buy your new machine or build real estate.  Write the computer program.

Many times you will need to have more or different people involved at this stage.  Many solutions will be company-wide or regional involving much more than buying one simple piece of equipment or special training for one or three people.  It is not unusual to need some solutions to happen before or after others.  There are entire books, courses and even college program majors in analyzing, scheduling and implementing projects.

5	Implement The Solution:  Put your solutions into effect.  Give your program to those who will use it. Turn that new machine on.  Move into your new offices.

6	Review And Revise:  It is VERY important to realize that you are not done yet even though this is step number 6, the last in the list.  In some ways this is the most important because it is the step most often overlooked.

> Yogi Berra,
> "It's not over til it's over."

Keep records of the results of your implementation of these solutions.  Analyze and compare your results with previous (pre-solution) information and with expectations.  Listen for squeaks, complaints or praise.

Repeat steps as needed on all or part of any of your solutions and their implementations.  The bigger the solution the more you need to closely monitor and revise as needed.

Be careful of System Tweaking, making changes just for the sake of change.  Realize that any process has variations larger and smallish.  Allow for them and get enough and accurate information to determine whether change is going to be needed.

An example of this might be an operator of the warming burner on a giant vat of chemicals. Let us say he wants the chemicals to come out of the vat at 75 degrees. He measures the temperature and finds it is 73 degrees so he raises the heat. Fifteen minutes later the outgoing temp is still 73 degrees so he bumps up the heat some more and leaves to do something else. Two hours later the chemicals are coming out at 85 degrees and the only provision for cooling is time. Everything has to stop and wait. What happened? What was overlooked?

> **Roadside Attraction 10**
>
> How many times should this operator have taken temperatures? How far apart?
>
> Write a hypothetical set of steps for one simpler solution.

This is an example of System Tweaking, over-tweaking in this case, based on insufficient information and imperfect sampling.

> **Roadside Attraction 11**
>
> Don't think you need this R&R step? When was the last time you did something where everything worked perfectly, fit exactly, came out exactly as planned? Be honest. PPP us detailing the success or disaster of a big plan you were involved in.

Have you noticed how it takes several minutes to boil water? It takes time to get enough heat distributed through the pan of water to raise the temperature. How much longer might a giant vat of

31

liquid take to raise its temp a few degrees? Probably longer than fifteen minutes?

Another example, often referred to as Super-Tweaking, would be when a big-deal auto exec drops by to inspect or tour a local plant making trucks. Let us say he sees 3 trucks with paint scratches and other obvious defects and decides to move the entire operation to another country since it is obvious this plant cannot adequately paint their trucks. Overreaction? Could our process be applied to find a simpler solution?

---

In his book, *Pudd'nhead Wilson*, Mark Twain created a calendar with a statement of monthly wisdom which included a relevant thought,

"A fool says don't put all your eggs in one basket. (You may recall the saying from Aesop's Fables.) A wise man says put all your eggs in one basket and WATCH that basket!"

---

Whatever your problem, you have invested a lot of time and effort so far in its solution. Keep your eye on it.

---

### Scenic Overlook

There becomes an art to applying our thinking rules, but like any art we first need to understand the basic rules.

Before you begin to try breaking or bending the rules you should make sure you have mastered them. Make sure you have created all of your PST cards, one for each rule, term and concept encountered so far. Review them all before continuing.

# Rules for breaking rules

We all know that breaking the rules is bad, isn't it? Rules are there to help. Always hold your partner's hand, never go swimming alone, never put beans up your nose, and rules such as that can help us get safely through the everyness of most days.

> **Scenic Overlook**
>
> Any rule-breaking process involves taking risks and should be only done initially in controlled conditions. Get some experience with driving short day trips on smooth roads before you try any of those fancy "Professional Driver, Closed Course" moves seen on TV.

Remember, if you already know how to solve the problem or answer the question then it is really more of an Exercise than a Problem. Also, if you could solve your problem using regular rules you probably wouldn't have a problem so much as another simple exercise. Rules often need to be broken or reshaped to fit new ideas and situations. Be prepared to question your own rules as well as others.

It turns out there are some rules for rule-breaking. We call this set of conditions and rules <u>Brainstorming</u>, <u>PST</u> <u>General</u> <u>Rule</u> <u>6</u>. Brainstorming is basically a set of rules for breaking the rules in a formal way that everyone can share and feel safe in both mind and job.

Brainstorming is done in many variations throughout the world of thinkers. Let us agree on a set of basic rules for our Brainstorming

sessions.  You can add or adapt as needed to individual companies or problems.
<u>Brainstorming</u> <u>Ground</u> <u>Rules</u>:

1) Free Exchange of Ideas:  Anyone can say anything without correction or derision from other participants.  This is important because we are asking people to take risks in front of peers or supervisors.  If there is fear of reprisal, even such small negative reinforcement as "boo" or "that's stupid" (how small are those really?) there can be no free exchange and all you will hear are pre-approved ideas.

> Yogi Berra, one of my personal favorite baseball players and accidental philosopher said,
>
> "Sometimes you can observe a lot just by looking."

If all you want to hear is old ideas then you are not Brainstorming you are simply recycling.  This doesn't mean that every idea has to be brilliant or even new.  Many times old ideas can be re-viewed in a different light to produce new and better results.

> **Roadside Attraction 12**
>
> PPP us on the ideas represented in the quote from Yogi and The lessons of The Emperor's New Clothes.  Do they give us any insights into thinking or into looking at ideas of our own or ideas presented by others?

2)  Consider All Viewpoints:  Make sure to give weight to all ideas not only the *good* ones.  This does not mean that every solution will contain every

> Side Trip:  Don't be afraid to state the obvious.  Do you know the story of The Emperor's New Clothes?  Share it with the class.

idea. It merely reinforces the ideal of Brainstorming which is to get new and different ideas and combinations of ideas on the table for consideration. If you refuse to consider these new ideas you defeat a major purpose of the Brainstorming method. If you are not looking for new ideas why are you Brainstorming?

3) Everyone Contributes: Get everyone to contribute at least one idea no matter how off-the-wall or ridiculous it might seem. Sometimes the most ridiculous idea can lead to the best solution.

Does anyone else recall the movie, Apollo 13, where the space capsule started leaking air halfway to the moon, "Houston we have a problem." In trying to brainstorm a solution one early comment was something to the effect that "If their ride's broken why don't they get out and walk home" as if that were an option like with a broken down car or truck. They couldn't walk home, of course, but it turned out they could get out of the leaking capsule and into their attached LEM, an act which ultimately saved their lives.

> Side Trip: In our software development team we have created a position named PSI, Professional Software Idiot. This person's job is to view the software from an innocent perspective with as few assumptions and prejudices as possible. It is often surprising what this perspective yields; it is always helpful to have this set of Innocent Eyes to keep you sharp and your product clean and functional.

4) Never Completely Discard Ideas: Never throw your ideas away. They may become useful at later stages of this problem solution or in the solution of another problem, perhaps completely unrelated at first to the current problem.

<u>Brainstorming</u> <u>Steps</u> may vary from textbook to textbook, but all represent the same philosophy of freedom of input to allow new solutions:

1) Setting: Get your group together in a non-judgmental, non-competitive environment with no distractions. This includes both attitude of participants and neutrality of location.

> Side Trip: Brainstorms often work better in some sort of Retreat setting. One large Toledo company had a tour bus made into a traveling conference room where all communications with the outside and therefore, day-to-day business matters, were made through a single executive assistant who was empowered to make interruptions only under the direst of circumstances. Sessions were scheduled for a specific number of hours with appropriate refreshment arrangements provided, thus meeting the Brainstorming requirements.

2) Discuss And Combine: Create and discuss everyone's ideas. When all ideas have been gathered begin to discuss each idea and any combinations of ideas that can be imagined. Same ground rules.

3) Get Practical: Finalize by asking practical questions and choosing those ideas which seem most valid or promising at the time. Also choose any ideas which sound as though they might be possibilities if more research supports

them.  These are your results of the Brainstorming session.  Some or all of these may be new to you or your company and require work to implement or expand into practical solutions.  Save all other ideas for future reference both in this project and in future projects or problem solutions.

In Brainstorming or other problem solutions don't forget the <u>Non-Solution</u> which is that case in which we do nothing.  In other words, is this problem something that will go away by itself in a reasonable amount of time?  For example, I hear an odd or unusual squeak in my car one morning.  Do I need to do something right away or can I simply wait until the car's next scheduled maintenance?  Different levels of sound intensity or strangeness might call for immediate actions, but some are simply <u>wait-and-see</u> problems.  We hear a form of this type of non-solution in the saying, often applied to children or second-childhoodlums in mid-life crisis, "It's just a phase!" meaning they'll get over their particular foolishness by themselves given time.  Sometimes the time taken to get over it is tolerable, other times action needs to be taken to move the person through the phase.

> **Scenic Overlook**
> of Non-Solution
>
> Conditions change. Appropriate non-solutions may call for radical innovation or may be the best ones for a long time.  That doesn't mean they should not be revisited periodically just like any other solution.

Side Trip: Businesses may have similar cycles. In Northern areas where winter's severe cold, snow and ice makes motorcycling less pleasant or even impossible for most folks. For decades motorcycle shops either shut down in the winter or cut back on staff and hours to make it through. They realized that summer would come again and decided it just wasn't worth it to spend money to try to promote business for winter when the problem would go away.

I picked the motorcycle industry on purpose because this non-solution to winter slow-down of business led to the creation of the recreational snowmobile. Some inventor re-asked the question of what motorcyclists do in the winter and came up with an answer different from the traditional "Sleep and Heal!" He came up with the concept of the recreational snowmobile, as opposed to the working tractor-type snowmobiles. Arctic snowmobiles were typically enclosed tractors with tank-like treads. This new "sled with a tread (belt)" was marketed to motorcycle dealers as an off-season moneymaker. Many dealers picked it up. Major motorcycle manufacturers began making snowmobiles. The snowmobile industry became as big or bigger than the motorcycle business.

Some dealers sold only snowmobiles, no motorcycles. This had a reverse effect, off-season in summer instead of winter. This problem got worse the farther south one went because there are actually more dry months than snowy months. The off or slow months were accepted as part of the industry. The next industry innovation was the jet-ski, in its basic concept a snowmobile that runs on water. Many dealers and manufacturers now have their line of both products.

**The Best Places to see:** Creative Thinking

You can be a creative thinker.

There is room and even need for creative thought and solutions in all areas of human endeavor. What-how-where is the beginning of <u>Creative</u> <u>Thinking</u>. To think creatively means to go where you have never gone before or even to think what no one has thought before.

OK, thinking creatively means to go where you have never gone before or even to think what no one has thought before. Sound scary? Sound like jumping off a cliff without a hang glider? Thinking creatively can be that exciting. Many people get hooked on the process itself and its application to a particular media for expression. We call them Artists or Poets or Songwriters or Visionaries or nutcases or weirdoes. Most of us really don't want to be classified as one or more of those things so we avoid creativity like the dis-ease it can be. It's OK to admit this.

> Scarifying
> Ain't it?

How can I convince you it is OK to be different? I cannot. I can only state it. You must decide that it is worth it or not. But let me add this: controlled creativity can make you a more valuable employee as well a more well-rounded person. Just because some may have carried creativity to illogical extremes does not mean you have to.

Songwriters and composers are all considered to be creative thinkers because their "solutions" are creations, they make something new from the old by creating different combinations or bringing things into being that never existed before.

> ### Roadside Attraction 13
>
> Consider these simple lines of poetry from Joyce Kilmer. "I think that I shall never see / A poem lovely as a tree." What do you hear in those lines? When was the last time you took a good look at a tree? Proceed to the closest tree in your mind and look at it for five minutes. Use a real tree or a picture of a tree. PPP what you see.

Poetry, song, literature, painting, and all forms of art allow us to see through other eyes, to experience things we may have never thought of or to think in ways we have never thought before. Sound like fun?

> ### Roadside Attraction 13A
>
> When was the last time you really looked at a tree? Next time you are sure no one is watching stand as close as possible to a large tree for a few minutes. Really look at the tree. Can you feel the life in the tree. hear its heart beating? Feel the flow of the sap? Write a poem or letter relating this experience to a friend. Then do it again pretending the friend has never seen a tree. How does that change your poem or letter?

Cultivating Inspiration, Intuition and insight

<u>Inspiration</u>: Merriam-Webster defines inspiration as, among other things, "the action or power of moving the intellect or emotions." One can be inspired by scenery, people or works of art. The question is, "what do you do with inspiration."

Or, more relevantly to our goals, "How do we apply this to enhance our Creative Thinking?"

> ### Roadside Attraction 14
>
> Consider the humbly magnificent sunset. Have you seen one? Is your attitude, "seen one seen them all?" When was the last time you were inspired by a sunset? What do people do when they are inspired by a sunset: paint pictures, take photos, meditate, drive off the road in rapturous abandon, complain when it hurts their eyes, or simply ignore it. Pick two of the previous possibilities or make up your own. PPP us explaining why, or why not, you would respond to a sunset that way.

Have you ever been inspired? For me inspiration tastes a lot like that first big-hill thrill on a roller coaster: Chemicals interact, changes happen, things drop out of normalcy and into something special and different enough to cause you to buy another ride ticket.

Can you learn to be inspired? Can you inspire or be inspired on command? I believe each of us has that awe and passion inside us and that we don't need to learn it. We only need to allow it to happen and to value it when it happens. I have had this confirmed in hundreds of workshops and performances.

> ### Scenic Overlook
>
> The term <u>Editor</u> will normally be used here to refer only to mental and abstract processes. <u>Autopilot</u> will refer to automatic physical processes such as walking, standing, breathing and sitting.

Many of us have had our inspiration devalued or suppressed until we cannot find it anymore. Thinking and working on it can help revitalize you.

Turn Off Your Editor

So how do we revitalize our inspiration? We simply need to learn to turn off our Editor, open our filters to let ideas flow and grow. What or who is my Editor? And how do I turn her/him off? Your Editor is that little person in your head who handles the huge amount of information flowing past your senses and sends you only those things that you need to consciously handle. (I know that you know there are no little persons living in your head. But it is often easier to think of The Editor as a person. Bear with me.) For most people this is so automatic they do not realize that they have an Editor. Some people seem to only be able to run on automatic with their Editor doing all the work. We all need some degree of Editor-Autopilot. Imagine for a moment how hard it might be to get around if you had to think fully about every single step you took.

How do you turn your Editor off? It is as easy as falling off a pie, to mix a couple of old saws.

> ### Roadside Attraction 15
>
> Have you ever injured a knee or ankle? Try to recall how this affected your walking. How long did it take to get used to the injury? Did it have to heal completely or did your Editor-Autopilot adapt quickly? PPP us sharing your experience.

There are many systems for doing this. Psychiatrists have exercises and tricks to get you to turn off your Editor. Volumes have been written to help musicians, artists, writers and poets to get to that place where they can be creative, by turning off their Editors. Many artists, and non-artists, feel compelled to use alcohol and other drugs to put their Editor to sleep so they can be inspired. Yoga, Tai Chi and most martial arts use physical and mental exercises to reach a meditation state, which involves turning off your Editor among other things. Hari Krishnas dance to achieve similar ends.

Psychoanalysis takes years. So do martial arts and Yoga. Drugs have serious consequences far beyond their benefits. So what can you do that doesn't take years or seriously kill you? It turns out that there are many small, quick exercises to help you get to your creativity. You have done many of them already. They are labeled "Roadside Attractions" in this book. No single exercise will work for every single person every time. Like most things you need several different repetitions (300-3000?) to master the process.

> Impatience is a virtue

You also need to have several different techniques for variety. If a process gets old it can lose its usefulness. Our methods can become jaded, like a knife that gets dull. We may need to switch tactics to resharpen our skills.

> Bustling Backwater: One technique to get by the Editor which I have used 20-25 times per year over the last decade with groups of all ages is a process I have named "Squish Art." (This process is detailed in my how-to book, *Squish Art, An Imagination Tool.*)

Personally I recommend exposing your self to as many thinking techniques and styles as you can, but concentrating on mastering one, then two, then three general approaches. Add more skills or more discipline-specific skills as you need them.

---

### Roadside Attraction 16

Try walking while concentrating on your feet. Try feeling your feet touch-press the ground as you walk. Feel it lift the heel to the toe. Try saying the process out loud as you walk. PPP us your feelings.

Can you turn off your Editor or Autopilot completely? Imagine what that would be like? Write it down without thinking or worrying about sentence or paragraph structure. Organize it as PPP and share.

Can you completely shut off all of your senses? Imagine what that would be like. PPP illustrating or explaining your idea of each sense or any combinations.

---

Do not forget, however, you need to be able to turn your filters or Editor back on as needed. We need our mental filters. They take care of all our regular needs. It would be impossible to drive a car, for example, if we had to make serious conscious note of every telephone pole, every line on the highway, every tree and bush, every blade of grass.

> Bustling Backwater: I once knew someone who worked with autistic children. As a consequence of our discussions on the subject of autism I have often wondered if a lack of the ability to filter could be central to that problem. Imagine what it might be like to have all the world competing equally for your attention every moment, all day, all night, all of the time.

The point is, don't throw Editors or Autopilots away, simply learn to turn them off when it is beneficial and appropriate.

> ### Roadside Attraction 17
>
> Did you know there was such a thing as a Sensory Deprivation Chamber that allows you, or forces you, to do just that? It cuts off all outside influences. Look up sensory deprivation and report your findings to the class or pair with a classmate. Revisit and rewrite your page on deprivation in light of your new information. Did you make major changes? Look at your first page describing full input. Does your information on Sensory Deprivation change or enhance those ideas? PPP responses.

What to do when you don't know what to do.

Sophisticated Wild Idea Guess (SWIG):  There are times when we have no real information to indicate one solution or solution path is the right one or even somehow a better one.  At this point you must build your own bridge to a new solution. One step is to simply make a guess.  One tries to make it a good guess, but if there is no real or hard information for us to go on it is often difficult to even rank guesses.  Therefore make your guess, let your unconscious make it for you.  Test it in as limited a fashion as possible for a valid try, limited especially in cost and time investment. Review the results including cost, consequences and potential.  Most times you will try several of these SWIGs before you come up with a good solution.

> Side Trip:  Why SWIG?  Well a swig is a quick, limited drink and this encompasses the basic idea of this tool.  Idea is what we are trying to get to solve our problem.  Wild is what our guess is.  Sophisticated describes us and the process if used correctly with conscious knowledge that we are only guessing to try something out.

Simple Idea Possibility (SIP):  When there is no solution path available, when even a sophisticated guess may be too much to ask for, start with a SIP.  SIPs are statements that begin with what-if, how-about, couldn't-we or remember-when.  Don't force them into ideas or solutions until you have considered them.

Insight

Merriam-Webster defines insight as "the power or act of seeing into a situation" or "the act or result of apprehending the inner nature of things or of seeing intuitively." That is, insight is a skill, but it is also an art; it is both a process and a path. We wish to develop our insight skills so that we can open up a problem or break down a problem into its basic parts and ideas.

There are some rules for promoting insight: Suspend disbelief/Suspend Belief; See With New Eyes; Bad rules, Bad!; Think Sideways; Why and why-not.

> Side Trip: A few decades ago, in my younger days, I read that one European country switched driving sides. They just decided that at a certain time everyone would drive on the other side. As I recall they chose a Friday at five PM which didn't make a bit of sense to me. I still hope that was a misprint or a mistranslation.

---

### Roadside Attraction 18

Get two or three people together and find something you believe automatically. This can be a touchy area since many beliefs stem from religion and from political ideas. So find an area where there is less volatility to begin with. One example is the idea of driving on the right side of the road. Is the right side the correct side? Why do we drive on the right in North America when a large part of the world drives on the left? PPP us. What time of day do you think would be best to change driving sides? What day? PPP us.

Suspend disbelief or belief:  If you are positive that a problem cannot be solved in a certain way then it is very unlikely that you would ask anyone to try that idea or method.

Have you ever been to a magic show?  Most of us are pretty sure that the lady doesn't actually turn into a tiger and back and that the magician does not tear up money and then restore it, but we can suspend disbelief and enjoy the illusions.  It is a bit tougher to suspend belief.

The statement "Dogs can't fly!" may get widespread agreement yet dogs were some of the first beings to fly into outer space.  There are special carriers and forms for when dogs fly on commercial aircraft.

If we want insight, if we desire a new perspective then it is important be able to set aside previous notions and yes-tions to see with new eyes.

So, rules are bad!  Not all rules are bad.  In fact most rules are there for pretty good reasons.  That does not mean all or any of those rules are currently valid or that they apply to this particular problem and its solution.

One of my favorite examples comes from *Whack on the Side of the Head.*  It tells of the case of a woman who always cooked a whole ham by cutting off a section at each end and pinning it to the top of the remaining ham with toothpicks.  The family referred to them as the "ears" if my memory is to be believed. When asked why she prepared her ham that way she said she never really thought about it. Her mother had done it that way and it worked just fine so she had continued the practice.

Can you guess what her mother's reply was when asked why she had done it that way? She said she had learned from her mother. When they finally got to the source of the process, the grandmother, they found out that she had trimmed the ends from the ham because her largest cooking pot wasn't wide enough to hold the whole ham and they couldn't afford to buy a bigger pot.

> **Roadside Attraction 19**
>
> Family stories are often interesting. Do you have a family tradition that is unusual or silly? Do you know where it came from? Ask your relatives to help pin it down.
>
> Can you think of a solution or problem where not-fixing might be the best answer? PPP to illustrate your tradition or solution.

It turns out that the granddaughter had the means to afford a larger cooking pot, but never even thought of that option because she was locked into a solution that worked. One popular rule which we have demonstrated here is "<u>If</u> <u>it</u> <u>works</u> <u>don't</u> <u>fix</u> <u>it.</u>" I agree that something that is working should not idly or whimsically be discarded, but that is not the same as saying that it cannot ever be thoughtfully challenged, reworked or even discarded.

It is important to be aware of your own inner rules and to be able to decide when they apply and when they do not. It is especially important to be conscious of other people's rules which may not apply at all or may even be wrong. We cannot count the times we have been corrected both rightly and wrongly by those around us, peers, parents, teachers and other authority figures. One directly injurious statement of this type which many of us have heard in its thousand variations is "You can't do that!" along with one of my most non-favorites, "You'll never amount to anything." The hurt from this type of negative feedback goes far beyond one simple moment

> Side Trip: I recall a young female student about twenty-five years ago who had serious problems thinking or doing math in any stress situation, but not intelligence problems. In working one-on-one I found out her story: It seems she had math problems in grade school so her father tried to assist by setting aside two hours after dinner to tutor her.
>
> The problem was that whenever she got a wrong answer he would call her stupid, sometimes even striking her in his frustration. If, on the other hand, she simply sat silent he would, after waiting about a minute, work the problem for her. Sadly, she was too agitated to follow his solutions, but she learned the lesson: if you shut up they won't hurt you.
>
> Before you judge the father too harshly realize that he had given a large piece of his own time in attempt to help his daughter. He was trying. Also realize that this is probably the way he learned from his father or teacher. It had worked for him.
>
> The point for our consideration though is that this student could make no progress on math until her basic method, fearful silent patience, was overturned completely. The catharsis involved tears, time, sympathy and practice, but she began to learn and finally got a bit better than average at math.

or statement. If it comes from authority figures or loved ones it can be seriously debilitating.

This type of sticking point or stumbling block happens in, one hopes, a less traumatic way for most of us at some point in our education,

> Side Trip: A friend and fellow poet told the story of his grade school art teacher admonishing him that "Blue and green never go together." When he told his mother after school she immediately asked, "Has that woman ever been outside?" Partially as a result of this my friend had both an artistic bent his whole life a healthy disrespect for those who were overly convinced of their authority.

whether in thinking or in some other discipline. We have other, perhaps less obvious <u>conceptual</u> <u>blocks</u> as well. These are things we hold so deeply that they never occur to us to question. These can often be conceptual blocks to creative thinking since they affect the way we see and think without our conscious knowledge.

If we are paying attention we often reach a point where these basic assumptions about things are challenged. I call this the <u>Everything</u> <u>I</u> <u>Know</u> <u>Is</u> <u>Wrong</u> point. Such conflict is an indication that you are ready to learn something new, that your world view is about to expand. This doesn't mean, of course, that everything we know is wrong, but rather that it is incomplete. This is something we must learn to deal with.

> Everything I know is WRONG!

> One definition of intelligence is the ability to hold conflicting ideas in mind at the same time.

Adjusting to new ways of thinking can be as painful as those first few weeks of a new exercise regimen but are often even more rewarding. After a few thousand times it starts to become natural. Do not be afraid to examine your own rules and ideas with a <u>why</u> and <u>a</u> <u>why not</u> question session.

> Bustling Backwater: I have had occasion to tutor many members of my extended family over the last three or four decades. My favorite comment came from a close cousin, a teenaged boy of seventeen at the time. When asked by his father how our tutoring sessions were going my student replied, "My head is bigger! And it hurts a little."

### Scenic Overlook

You need to identify your personal rules, opinions and prejudices. You need to be prepared to modify those rules, opinions and prejudices or set them aside if it becomes necessary. Flexibility of mind is a major goal. You often need to take the personal rules, opinions and prejudices of others into account in your solutions.

Why will something work? How does it work? What do I really see going on here? Remember Yogi Berra's, "Sometimes you can observe a lot just by looking." Open your eyes. Really look. Truly see what you look at. Apply this liberally to your own mind.

### Roadside Attraction 20

Think back along your learning journey. Maybe even this very book could have pushed you, or maybe challenged you, to rearrange your ideas and methods. PPP us a version of that experience. Did it cause pain or exasperation? Satisfaction?

Relax your mind. Think straight. Expand your borders. Think sideways. This idea of <u>Sideways or Lateral</u> <u>Thinking</u> can be related to our PSTGR1, Given-Known-Need, in that this is merely an extreme example of what we know. To say it another way we almost always know more than we need to solve a particular problem.

> **Scenic Overlook**
>
> Lateral is a widely used British term. See Resources for Lateral Thinking problem/puzzle books.

Sideways thinking reminds us to look in different directions and bring different, seemingly unrelated knowledge and skills to our problem.

<u>Crazy</u> <u>Thinking</u>: Make a leap. Have you ever found yourself saying "That will never work." or "No one would ever . . ." or "How can you even think such a thing?" These are indications that you are approaching crazy thinking. Every great idea was labeled crazy when it was first put forth. Let your Crazy Person sing (but don't let them drive your car).

> **Roadside Attraction 21**
>
> My grandfather loved his stories about outrunning automobiles as a kid in 1908 to 1913. The young men used to run backwards in front of the cars and shout, "Get a horse!" Hey, they didn't have TV or even radio back then. PPP a vision of what your life would be if there were no TV or Radio or Internet. No cars or airplanes?

Side Trip: I often played catcher on my baseball teams growing up. I recall a particular dropped third strike that I lost sight of. I jumped up and looked around in every direction several times. Typically one's teammates will shout encouragement and helpful hints in a situation like this.

My teammates, the umpire, the spectators and even my own father were laughing so hard they couldn't speak. I guess the picture I presented hopping as fast as I could in a circle in full catcher's gear trying to find the dropped ball was so comical they couldn't overcome their laughter.

The umpire limited the runners to one base because it was "a situation beyond human control," the same rule they invoke if a dog steals the ball or a pigeon hits the ball to make it uncatchable.

It turns out the ball was resting quite comfortably between my feet the entire time I was turning and jumping. I was even, inadvertently, picking it up with my shoes when I hop-turned.

## Scenic Overlook

If you cannot, or will not, see the solution then it doesn't matter if it is right under your nose or caught between your toes.

Look everywhere. Look where you would never think to look. Completely see what you look at. Do not be afraid to examine what you know as true. Always be prepared to see differently when looking regularly.

## Roadside Attraction 22

"You always find something in the last place you look." Is this true? Why is that? If this is true why don't we look there first? PPP us on this applied to some human condition such as love or marriage.

# Consider Go-ghoti – Language Puzzler

Ghoti is another way of spelling the fish. On a Google search the word ghoti got 30,400 hits. Never heard of it? George Bernard Shaw first invented or discovered the word ghoti with the gh from laugh, the o from women and the ti from nation and pronounced "fish" as an example of our strange English language. (note: Some sources say Shaw actually got the ghoti spelling from some, now unknown, advocate of spelling reform and simply made it popular.) What in the world does this idea mean? Don't we already have a perfectly good word for fish? Why would someone invent another?

> **Bustling Backwater:** Can you believe there are scholars and people taking time to think about this word or non-word. Did you know there has been a movement across the English-speaking world to simplify or standardize spelling?
>
> Oddly enough many people when discussing this word often pronounce it as "goaty" to make sure listeners know what form they are talking about. I even heard one learned speaker use the term goaty-fish to refer to it in a discussion.
>
> PPP us using goaty-fish. Can goaty-fish swim? Are they amphibious? What would a goaty-fish look like? Scales or fur? Maybe both? How long do goaty-fish live? Are they happy? Do they believe themselves to be beautiful? Does a ghoti-fish suffer from schizophrenia?

> **Roadside Attraction 23**
>
> Write three paragraphs or so telling why you think Shaw would create such a word and what it implies for us today. Make up five new spellings for familiar words on your own using Shaw's method. Share them with the class.

The basic idea of creative thinking is simply to look at something differently. A creative thinker looks at the same thing as everyone else and sees something different.

Another Creative thinking technique is to stand your problem on its head. For example, if your problem is how to get people to love your new product and you are having trouble with ways to do that (Yes, I too am wondering why we are making something no one really wants, but that does seem to be rather a wide-spread practice nowadays.) try turning the problem down-side up: "How can we get people to hate this product so much they will buy multiple copies so they can burn them with their neighbors in midnight bonfires."

---

### Roadside Attraction 24

Try to make up a product that is so undesirable that it would fit this scenario. PPP. Look at it this way. Close one eye. Close both eyes and see with your ears. Try standing on your head? If you are physically unable to do this use a mirror to see everything downside up. PPP something that has turned your world view up-side-down.

**Drive This Way**: The Art of Thinking

The Art of Thinking involves when to use and when not to use which tools, and how to apply them to best advantage each time. Can you accept that this takes time and practice to master? The art of thinking is to master the techniques and to learn to apply them to different situations with ease.

> Side Trip: Picasso (famous artist in case you didn't know; my spell checker doesn't) was once asked in a TV interview how he was able to paint so quickly and accurately. Some of his most interesting works are paintings with one or a very few brushstrokes that yet somehow create an image of depth and interest. Picasso replied that one simply sees whatever image one desires in his head and then projects it on the canvass where he copies it. Sound easy? I think he practiced more than 3000 times. Maybe he was born with that gift. I am pretty sure that, in his case, it involves liberal portions of each.
>
> Related: A famous sculptor was asked how he could create such lively images from dead rock. His response has become a classic in art circles, "If you want a sculpture of an elephant you just take your block of marble and chip away everything that doesn't look like an elephant!"

Applying thinking tools and processes is the province of the Critical Thinker. How do you become a Critical Thinker? Are all artists Critical Thinkers? Are all Critical Thinkers artists?

> Side Trip: One interesting idea on thinking was popularized in a movie, *The Heist,* with lines given by actor Gene Hackman. His character was asked how he came up with his brilliant ideas when he seemed so normal, even stupid, at times. He informed us that, "When I get a problem I can't solve I just imagine a man twice as smart as I am and think how he'd do it."

Not at all.  Many modern artists think of themselves as interpreters or arbiters of popular rhythms trying to portray emotions more than ideas or information.  Some are even anti-thinking, at least on a conscious level, in their art or about their works.  Many successful computer programmers and mathematicians never even feel the desire to create conventional art.  Some are very creative within their areas, but not outside of that.

> **Roadside Attraction 25**
>
> We all have artistic senses and abilities.  Many of us have allowed them to languish or even wither.  Several colleagues insist that our school system is geared to crushing the art out of us.  They posit that this happens by the third grade in most cases.  In other words, we have already decided by then who is an artist, singer, athlete etc. and that it is clearly marked on your permanent record by conscientious elementary educators.  Can you recall an experience where you were discouraged from participation in a play, contest or sport by an official?  PPP your feelings and details then and now.

> **Roadside Attraction 26**
>
> Is this art?  Not as easy as you might have believed?  Is art in the eye of its creator or, like beauty, in the eye of the beholder?  Where is beauty?  Want to toss in Truth while we're at it?  PPP on Truthless Art and Beauty.  Did I mention that the cat-art book reported that one of the featured cats had sold a painting for $15,000 just before that book went to press?

Some artists do not think at all, at least in any human sense.  Have you heard about cat artists?  Elephant artists?  Some zookeeper came up with the idea of giving an elephant a paintbrush and having it "paint pictures."  It made a great exhibit and, according to the keepers, the elephant enjoyed it.  It wasn't long before human people decided that those paintings were worth money which was used to help the zoo.  One can only hope the elephant got some of the money as well.  There is a book on cat art, both the process and some examples.  Tip one:  make sure the cat is declawed.

The only requirement for being a thinker is to think.  The only requirement for being a writer is to write.  However, we often make a huge distinction between someone who writes paragraphs and some-other-one who writes novels.  There is also a difference in most people's minds between a novelist and a great novelist.  Can we apply that idea to thinking.

How do you tell the difference between levels of thinking?  How can you tell who is a Thinker and who is a Critical Thinker?  Let's try on a common definition and see if it fits.  Let us say that a Thinker is someone who knows thinking rules and can apply them when required.  A Critical Thinker then is a Thinker who applies those rules to all situations without being asked.

> Side Trip:  I'll also accept applying thinking to most situations without being asked, since there are any number of everyday areas where conscious critical thinking is rarely called for, breathing for example.

Another part of the art of thinking is the ability to see different viewpoints, even to embrace them completely on a temporary basis as if they were your own. I call this seeing through someone else's eyes.

> ### Roadside Attraction 27
>
> When I worked as an electrician I used to make mental note of electrical details such as switch height and placement and the number of outlets in a room. Walk out of the room and walk back in looking and thinking as if you were an electrician. Try it as a firefighter. Choose any other discipline or training and use those eyes. PPP us on each and on the combinations. How about having each person write down a profession and mixing them in a hat? Everyone could then pick a random profession from the hat and try to use those eyes to see the room.

> ### Scenic Overlook
>
> A large part of becoming a Thinker is learning the rules and concepts. Most of the road to becoming a Critical Thinker is putting thinking to work on a regular basis until it becomes part of your world view.

So how can we apply our thinking rules and ideas? How can we apply this Thinking Art? The first and most important step is to feel the need or desire. The second is to throw away your fears of thinking, of being bad at it or of looking foolish to peers or supervisors.

> Side Trip: Try using your brain and applying this critical thinking thing for ninety days. If you are not completely satisfied we will sadly, but surely, refund your brain.

So why aren't all Critical Thinkers <u>Great</u> <u>Thinkers</u>? One major difference is that a great thinker takes on bigger problems on a regular basis and succeeds to some meaningful degree. Not all thinkers apply or need to apply their talents to

> **Roadside Attraction 28**
>
> Think of a solution you have thought up for a problem at work, home or school. PPP it.

> Side Trip: Not all solutions are implemented. I remember the story from a Toledo, Ohio plant that manufactured spark plugs. It seems that there was a place on the production line where there was a consistently high level of breakage. The sparkplugs dropped too far from one conveyor belt to the next and often cracked or broke their ceramic portions and therefore had to be reworked or discarded. Management decided it would cost more to rearrange the lines and machinery than they lost so they decided to do nothing.
>
> A millwright or a machine operator (stories vary), made an odd-shaped basket that swiveled and slid to collect a few dozen sparkplugs about halfway down and then to dump them relatively softly onto the lower belt. This resulted in almost no breakage or damage to the plugs. Workers actually cheered as they saw the test work. They knew that every broken plug cost them and the company money.
>
> Our hero's next move seems a bit odd in retrospect. After a brief nod of acknowledgement he disassembled his solution and cut it to pieces, stating that he wasn't going to give it to the company for nothing and the company had no policy or history of rewarding innovations. The problem continued even though a solution existed.

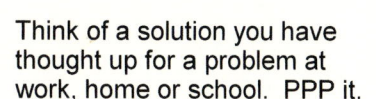

great problems. We have had many great thinkers in our world history. We can build on their solutions and mimic their processes to a large degree. It is often the case that reasonable solutions are discounted because of special, vested interests or general prejudice.

> Bustling Backwater: It is one sad footnote to history that the inventor of blood plasma died from blood-loss from a car accident outside a hospital that wouldn't admit him because of the color of his skin. Afterwards everyone involved agreed that a plasma transfusion could have saved his life. Challenge your prejudices on a regular basis.

## **Future Journeys**:
## Discipline-Specific Thinking Tools

Specialized thinking

In most areas of expertise there are specialized thinking vocabularies and concepts. After successfully completing the previous portions of this booklet the student should have a good foundation to successfully build upon for any specialized area. Many of these skills and concepts should be added to any serious thinker's toolbox. Others are of interest only to specialists in a particular area. Collect them all and use what you need.

---

**Roadside Attraction 29**

List six categories of tools you think should work for your particular major or occupation. Make dividers for your PST Toolbox with those titles on them. Feel free to make new ones or add new tools to sections where they seem to fit.

---

Side Trip: How many tools do you own? My garage has half-dozen power tools and more than a baker's dozen toolboxes. If I want to work on pipes I reach first for the plumbing toolbox and then for the general tools. I also have a huge toolbox to hold other toolboxes.

How to keep track? Which box to grab when? The trick is to organize things so you know where they are and how to use each one. Another part is remembering names and uses of each toolbox and all the tools inside. . .

Wait a minute! Could this system apply to our PST Toolbox as well. Could one PST Toolbox section be labeled "general" and another "Programming?" Another might be labeled "Engineering" or "Social Sciences" or "Biology" or . . .

In some disciplines or specialties the basic thinking rules given in this book are restated or adapted to better shape the problem solving thinking to their traditional problem types. This means that computer people are trained to solve problems that have often cropped up in computers and architects are trained to solve problems associated with designing buildings. After a brief moment of reflection does that sound like a good idea?

However, if you observe different problem solvers and thinkers from different training or educational backgrounds you will also notice that those individuals often have very different perspectives on the world and often use widely separated methods of thinking and problem solution.

> Bustling Backwater: In the sixties there was an author and scientist named C.P. Snow who wrote many articles and books on this basic problem, especially as it existed between his two worlds, Novelist and Scientist. He warned against the problems that such a gulf might mean for the future of our world. If all common ground is eliminated and scientists and artists couldn't communicate at all where would we end up?
>
> Snow lobbied for a scientific and engineering education that included writing, literature and history, as well as a liberal arts education that included science and engineering training.

This is not yet bad either taken by itself, but Sometimes serious problems arise when different individuals cannot see the viewpoint of the others. This can be a problem.

Many times it is this specialized training which has them locked into one perspective or solution. Sometimes you have to be willing to go back to basic thinking rules and techniques, such as breaking your own thinking rules to be able to see from another perspective.

---

### Roadside Attraction 30

Do you know anyone who has a viewpoint or thinking process that is severely limited by their own way of thinking? PPP.

---

### Scenic Overlook

I would strongly recommend to students that they continue using their PST toolbox and to expand it into subsequent subject areas. My own organization would be to classify those cards into those tools that apply only to that specific area and those that are really expansions or extensions of those foundation skills we have learned and practiced here.

Mathematical Thinking

Geometry-style formal proof involves step-by-step progress from a known truth to a desired conclusion with every step justified by a valid, logical reason, normally expressed in the form of an axiom or corollary. In Geometry these reasons are called postulates, the basic assumptions of our Plane Geometry system, and axioms, those truths which can be proved from the postulates. Once something is formally proved it can them be used as a reason for a step in another formal proof. Reductio Ad Absurdum means to carry your idea or hypothesis out to its next logical step and its next and its next using formal proof methodology. If you finally get to something you can prove is absolutely wrong then your initial hypothesis is false.

Deductive Reasoning and Inductive Reasoning are both techniques that have been used for centuries by mathematicians and are widely validated and accepted. Deductions are based on facts we know that are put together to prove something we guessed should be true, very much like the formal Geometry-style proof. Induction is a form of proof where we look at one Base case and then build the proof by making a general proof of the Next Case. That is, if a given base case is true and if the general statement for any next case is true then the proof is true for all such cases.

Scientific Thinking

Practical skepticism, a mindset that accepts nothing as true without proof. See Scientific Method. Also uses all types of problem solving and logic.

Philosophical Thinking:  Formal Logic

Syllogisms are a formal series of statements leading to a logical conclusion. For example, all tall men are good basketball players. Bill is tall. Therefore Bill is a good basketball player. If we accept the first two statements as true the third follows as true. In this case we know that not every tall man is a good basketball player. So even if Bill is tall it does not guarantee that he is a good basketball player. If either of the first two statements is false we have no proof of our conclusion.

Another tool of logic is the finding of Fallacies with such names as Circular Logic, God Said Arguments, Bandwagon, Bad Source, Ad Hominem. These should be added to most thinkers' toolboxes, but are covered in other texts.

| This statement is false |

Propositional and prepositional calculus are two very powerful logical tools. Such systems can be set up to handle almost any system of statements and ideas. One interesting consequence of these formal logic systems is

Goedel's Incompleteness Theorem which proves the limits of any such formal system. These are advanced studies for most, but we may see their roots in Boolean Algebra and Venn Diagrams covered in many college algebra courses.

Computer Programming Thinking

Syntax Rules for programming give the basic grammar for a programming language. Algorithmic Logic is the common computer sense used to design program flow.

Rules for deductive thinking very similar to those used in math and formal logic are useful to the computer programmer.
Your Computer Toolbox is that set of rules, definitions and concepts used to create programs.

OOP thinking, the concepts of classes, inheritance and other Object Oriented Programming skills allow the programmer to create modern OOP programs.

Thinking like the computer. Thinking and non-thinking like a user to anticipate user expectations.

Recursive thinking is a method of programming allowing a routine to recall itself again and again until it has reached some predefined state and then fold all of the calls into a single answer. Not all languages allow this.

Fuzzy Logic encompasses the idea of letting the computer make guesses. It is usually extended to allow the computer program to learn from those guesses to make better guesses in the future.

Engineering Thinking

Don't assume! Reminds the engineer to challenge basic assumptions in all engineering situations.

Murphy's Law: "If anything can go wrong it will go wrong and at the worst possible moment."
Corollary: Murphy was an optimist.
One rivet-bolt-screw doesn't weigh much. A few thousand add up quickly. Don't forget to sweat the details.

Art & Creative Thinking

Crazy thinking & Brainstorming are tools used regularly if not formally in art circles. Let your crazy person paint/write/perform.
Trying again with different tools or mixing tools that are normally not associated with one another such as painting with your toes or a cat's toes.

Use tools designed for one task to do another such as painting with a violin bow while playing a Bach Fugue.

Give your editor a name and invite him to lunch. Getting to know your editor and blind spots.

See what you look at means simply seeing with New Eyes or Innocent Eyes.

See everything differently today is a way of reminding yourself to not be satisfied with your personal limitations in thinking or creativity.

---

### Scenic Overlook

These are only some samples of other systems or disciplines of thinking. These broad samples should give you some idea of the methods and concepts open to you now that you have begun your long journey by completing this foundation journey.

Maybe you would like to go back and try Roadside Attraction 00 now. See if it makes more sense or if there is some sense hidden there which was not obvious before you reached your current level of PST skills.

---

### Roadside Attraction 00

Remember this one?

List ten reasons why *THINK* may be considered a 4-letter word.

List ten reasons why *LOVE* is not a 4-letter word.

## After-word

So our journey is ended; we stand challenged, exercised and winded.  Ready for our rest.  Right?

Sorry, Folks!  If you have been following carefully you probably are already aware that this is just the first step on a life-long journey.  If that sounds unpromising just remember that those skills captured in your Thinking Toolbox are yours for life.  The more you apply these skills the better you will become at solving problems and thinking critically and creatively in all areas of your life.

Congratulations on making that first giant step.  Is your brain bigger?   I hope it doesn't hurt too much.

> **Final?**
> **Roadside Attraction**
>
> PPP a summary of your feelings and achievements.  Print a copy of it and put it in your PST Toolbox.

> **Home Alonely Roadside Attraction**
>
> Imagine for three or four minutes that you can actually hear what is going on around you, everything that is going on everywhere around you. Close your eyes. Breathe fully, but gently. Move as little as possible. Can you hear your heart? Can you hear others in the room breathing? Are there people in another room? A radio or TV? Distant wind or weather? floors or chairs creaking?
>
> Does any unusual sound come alive? Anything you never heard before? When you wrinkle your nose does it make a sound? Did you find any sounds you never heard before? PPP.

**Appendix A**: Creating Your Thinking Toolbox

The PST ToolCard

Orientation: What the wonderment is a ToolCard? Even my spellchecker doesn't recognize this term! That's cause I made it up. A PST ToolCard is the place for you to record each new Thinking Skill as soon as you get it. The resulting set of PST ToolCards is your Thinking ToolBox. PST stands for Problem Solving Thinking which is where we are going with all this thinking talking we are doing.

"A poor workman always blames his tools" is a widely used criticism for someone who has problems, but if you don't have good tools to work with it is not easy to do a good job on any skill-based task whether carpentry or architecture to name two ends of a design process. You need to be quite skilled to perform high quality work with low quality tools; it is much better to have quality tools and learn to use them. We hope that these PST ToolCards will work as high quality tools as you begin to master them by first copying and learning their theory and then applying it to different situations.

Explanation of Card fields:

Name Student Name: Print your name.
ToolCard #: The number given by this text for this Thinking Skill.

Type  The name of the category this Thinking Skill fits into. How have we classified this skill in relation to the others.

Title/Subject:   The name of this skill.
Page  write down the page number from this text where you found the information or definition on this skill. There might eventually be more than one page number here.

Text: This is a reference to the textbook or reference book you got the tool info from. For this Text HTT stands for How To Think, the subtitle of this text.

Steps:    Write down the primary steps to accomplish this skill. Normally there should be 5 or less of these per skill. If there are too many you might need to break the skill or concept down more or simply use another card and staple them together.

Questions: List the questions involved. Number them if they need to be asked in order. Try to keep it to 3 or less. If there are too many you might need to break the skill or concept down more or simply use another card and staple them together.

Comment: What else do you want to remember in relation to this skill. One example might be to reference another skill that should be accomplished before beginning this one.

The Card:

| PST | | |
|---|---|---|
| Name: _____ ToolCard #____ Type: _____ | | |
| Title/Subject: _____ | Page: _____ Text:: HTT | |
| Steps (5-6 optimum) | Questions (3 max) | |
| | Comment: | |

**Appendix B**: Thinking Styles

There are many different styles of thinking; I believe every single person who thinks has their own style.  There are several widely agreed upon classes listed below.  There are also tests to see which class you fall into.  This doesn't mean that you only think in one way, it just shows your current dominant style which can change as you become a more proficient thinker.  Here are some widely recognized Thinking Style Categories:

> Have Brain Will Think

      Existential thinker
      Interpersonal thinker
      Kinesthetic thinker
      Linguistic thinker
      Logical-Mathematical thinker
      Musical thinker
      Naturalistic thinker
      Renaissance thinker
      Spatial thinker

There are also books out there hoping-helping you to think like great historical thinkers such as Mozart, Einstein, or Da Vinci.  Once you have mastered basic foundation tools these books and their perspectives can be helpful in forming your individual style.  It is not the goal of this text to explain or expand on these, merely to point out future thinking journey possibilities, much as a friend might say you must see the whales on your trip to Cape Cod.  Enjoy the whales.

**Appendix C**: Suggested Pedagogy

It is expected that this text is part of a thinking class or a thinking portion of an introductory discipline class. The basic presentation plan is to use that time on the first day of class when most students are ill prepared for any discussion of the subject matter to introduce basic concepts and overview of this system, filling in one or more PST cards and working on that process so students are ready to work through the text on their own. In subsequent classes ten to thirty minutes of discussion should be spent on these exercises, the Roadside Attractions, presented herein to keep students conscious of both process and importance of thinking skills. Depending on student reading levels and previous experience, exercises should be assigned as homework allowing and requiring students to think for themselves, report to the class and carry their own weight in class discussions. Startup thinking sessions also generate enthusiasm and energy for the rest of the class period.

It is beneficial to provide puzzle-type problems in addition to the included exercises for the class to solve. I have successfully used discussion threads on the web to pose a problem and encourage student participation outside of class. In most cases students were willing, even eager to provide their own problems for classmates to solve after the first few classes. See the lateral thinking books in Resources for sample problems or surf the web. Students, if you are working with those books on your own make a point of not looking at the solutions for several days (two or three) because benefit from these problems is in the thinking process as much, or more than the solution.

It is important that the instructor make conscious reference to PST skills in any other work where thinking or problem solving is required and have students create toolcards for discipline-specific skills. This can and should be carried into subsequent courses, providing a common learning tool and a consistent thinking vocabulary for students and teachers.

Take **special note** of the additional Roadside Attractions in Appendix D. These are provided for teachers who might like to substitute some of those for the numbered Roadside Attractions as well as for further exploration by students. For the final week's thinking assignment in my classes I ask students to create three to five of their own Roadside Attractions using these and the sample Road Signs for example and inspiration.

**Appendix D**:  More Thinking Road Signs &
           Roadside Attractions

Road signs on your thinking journey are statements that make you think, things or ideas that make you go HMmmm . . . ?

Road signs:

How high is up?                          Seven is jealous five
Don't even think about it!
Five is jealous of nine.
Nine hates ten.
This statement is true
Don't think!  Just do it.                Think!
Spaghetti for our national bird
Zamboni for president                    Make love not war
Newspeak news
I can see me and it ain't pretty
Love isn't                               Range cattle at large
Scream of consciousness
Too far for you?
Let your crazy person sing               Clean your filters
Moonlight Tavern                         Filters are for wimps
Turn off your editor Warning!            Will work for puns
Critical Thinker inside
Stop juggling your mental blocks
If I had enough money I'd be rich.
If I were taller I wouldn't be so short.
Crazy people have a good head start

bird tattoos:
> Live to fly . . . fly to live
> Fly or die
> South my feathered butt  (on a militant non-migrator?)
> Florida or bounce
> Why is there air?
> On a sparrow's wing:  five eagle silhouettes crossed
>> out
> I spent four months in Key West and all I got was this
>> lousy tattoo
> I'm not sad I've got clouds in my eyes.

dog tattoos:
> Ruff Stuff
> Here Kitty!
> Catch my tail
> Dogs Rule Cats Drool
> Fetch This
> Lapsitter
> Born to Hunt
> Pack It
> I Howled at Bubba's

Roadside Attractions are more ideas for extra practice of your thinking skills.

## Roadside Attractions:

Make up your own (10) silly saying road signs.
Pick two poems and try to make them into one.
Make up a silly song helping kids to think.
Try not to think of a brown dog for five minutes.
Write a job description for your perfect job.
Pick a favorite color. Explain what it does on its day off. Why?
Pick a place to be from. Explain why.
If birds gave milk and cows flew what difference would that make?
Tell about your ugliest/worst day.
If you could make one invention just for you what would it be?
Pretend you are you favorite animal.
Spend five minutes examining your knuckles with a magnifying glass.
What would the world be like if horses flew?
What would your life be like if money grew on trees?
Tell about your happiest or best day.
What one invention to help the world you wish for?
What would the world be like if you could read everyone else's mind.
Pretend everyone knows everything about you for twenty seconds?
Make funny faces at yourself in the mirror every morning for a week.
    Did it affect your attitude? Did you enjoy it?
Open a book of quotations to a random quote. Write a response or
    explanation.
Open your mind for 72 seconds every night before you go to bed.
    Write down what you see or feel.
Pretend to sleep and dream for five minutes;
    tell what you didn't dream about.
Sit alone for five minutes with a friend and try to be quiet enough to
    hear each other's heartbeats.
Sit in a grassy park to watch the sun go down or come up.
What would you do if you walked onto an elevator and everyone in it
    was facing the wall?
Find a friend; try not to laugh while making your friend laugh.

**Appendix E**: List of PST Rules

General Thinking Rules

| # | Name | Page |
|---|---|---|
| 1 | Given-Known-Needed | 18 |
| 2 | Scientific Method | 23 |
| 3 | Create Smaller Problems | 25 |
| 4 | Seeing the same, but different | 26 |
| 5 | Formal Problem Solving Steps | 28 |
| 6 | Brainstorming Rules & Method | 34 |

Creative Thinking Rules

| # | Name | Page |
|---|---|---|
| 1 | Turn off your Editor | 42 |
| 2 | Suspend Belief or Disbelief | 48 |
| 3 | New or Innocent Eyes | 48 |
| 4 | Bad Rules, Bad! | 48 |
| 5 | Why and why not | 52 |
| 6 | Think Sideways | 53 |
| 7 | Crazy Thinking | 53 |

# Glossary of Important Terms

| | |
|---|---|
| 3000 Times Rule | It takes approximately 3000 repetitions for an idea, action, rule or deed to become automatic. |
| Art Of Thinking | Involves when to use and when not to use which thinking tools and how to apply them to best advantage each time. |
| Brainstorming | An idea generation process wherein an open, non-threatening, non-judgmental atmosphere can lead to innovative or creative thinking and problem solution. |
| Brainstorming Ground Rules | A set of rules leading to successful new idea generation. See index for page number of steps and rules. |
| Brainstorming Steps | A set of steps leading to successful idea generation. See index for page number of steps and rules. |
| Bustling Backwater | A marker created for this booklet to indicate a topic or idea which might or might not seem relevant to the beginning student at that time, but which should be both relevant and interesting at some point to many, if not most, successful thinkers. It is left to the Guide (instructor) and the Traveler (student) to decide the which and when of these on each journey through this landscape. |
| Cheating | Taking shortcuts in problem solving by getting outside help. Sometimes this is the best solution. |
| Comprehension - Conscious | Conscious Comprehension is the Zone or state of understanding a task or concept and being able to perform or explain it successfully, but only with conscious thought or awareness of the tasks involved. See Comprehension – Unconscious. |
| Comprehension - Unconscious | Unconscious Comprehension is the Zone or state of understanding a task or concept and being able to perform successfully without thinking about it. The task is mastered and automatic. In some cases the person who has reached this state finds it so automatic that she/he has difficulty thinking or explaining the steps involved. Consider the task of walking. See Comprehension – Conscious. |

| | |
|---|---|
| Conceptual Block | These are things/ideas we hold so deeply that it never occur to us to question them. These can often be blocks to creative thinking since they affect the way we see and think without our conscious knowledge. |
| Conscious Thought | Those thought processes you need to think about to make happen as opposed to automatic or unconscious thought. |
| Corollary | This is a statement that follows from or relates to, sometimes modifies, a rule statement. In formal logic it is provable (follows) from the main rule or axiom. |
| Creative Thinking | The process or manner of thinking creatively, tat is generating completely new ideas and solutions or blending ideas in new ways. Sometimes called artistic thinking or right-brained thinking. |
| Critical Thinking | The process of applying skills in an organized manner to a problem or situation. One can be classed as a critical thinker if they regularly apply their thinking skills to problems or situations in or out of the classroom. |
| Everything I Know Is Wrong | In thinking and learning we often reach a point where our basic assumptions about things are challenged. I call this the Everything I Know Is Wrong point. Such conflict is an indication that you are ready to learn something new, that your world view is about to expand. |
| Exercise | A set of needs or situations which we have encountered before in very similar combination and, therefore, are only required to apply known, practiced rules or algorithms to successfully negotiate or solve. See Old Problem. |
| Human Learning Rule | Rules or concepts for the way we learn something. |
| If it works don't fix it | This refers to the idea of rejecting change. Good if applied to change for the sake of change. We should be prepared to question this as well if needed. |
| Incomprehension | The Zone or state of not understanding a task or concept. |

| | |
|---|---|
| Lateral Thinking | Lateral, or Sideways, Thinking is an extreme example of what we know. We almost always know more than we need to solve a particular problem. Sideways thinking reminds us to look in different directions and bring different, seemingly unrelated knowledge and skills to our problem solution process. |
| New problem | That class of problem where you have never seen it or anything like it; maybe you have never even thought about the concepts involved. Not only is some information missing, but so are some or even all of the basic concepts. See Problem. |
| No-Brainer | A problem so simple or familiar that there is almost no conscious thought needed. Also used to indicate a choice with such obvious solution. If something is a No-Brainer there is probably no real problem, perhaps merely a simple exercise. The problem is when we mistake a complex problem for a No-Brainer. |
| Non-Solution | That type of problem that will clear itself up in a reasonable amount of time. See Wait-and-See. |
| Old Problem | That class of problem that we have seen before and solved successfully many times. The missing information in the problem is well known to us and we probably need to do little or no involved thinking to get the information and the desired answer. See Exercise. |
| PPP | This is an acronym created for this book. It stands for page, poem or picture. It indicates that you should feel free to respond in one of many ways including, but not limited to the aforementioned. For example you could also write and put a on a skit or one-act play. You could compose a song. Or create a Gregorian chant. Try them all. Make up your own. |
| Problem | A new set of needs or situations which we have never encountered before in precisely this combination and, therefore, are required to apply thinking and problem solving skills to successfully negotiate or solve. See New Problem. |

| | |
|---|---|
| Problem Angle | It is important to see that one basic problem can be viewed from many perspectives leaving in or out different information or imbedding it inside other levels of information so that it appears different to the casual observer. Looking from any of these Problem Angles one should be able to identify the basic or root problem. See Problem Root. |
| Problem Root | One problem can be viewed from many angles or options. It is an important skill in solving problems to identify the Root Problem and learn to solve that. Viewing new problems as simply variations on a root problem you already understand and can solve often leads smoothly to the solution of the new problem. See Problem Angle |
| PST | Problem Solving Thinking, the processes and skills we can use to solve problems. |
| PST General Rule 1 | The first rule and General attacking tool of PST: Given, Known, Need. |
| PST General Rule 2 | The second rule of PST: The Scientific Method. |
| PST General Rule 3 | The third rule of PST: Create Smaller Problems |
| PST General Rule 4 | The fourth rule of PST: Seeing the same, but different |
| PST General Rule 5 | The fifth rule of PST: Formal Problem Solving Steps |
| PST General Rule 6 | The sixth rule of PST: Brainstorming Rules & Method |
| PST Toolbox | Both a metaphor for all the tools you have and a name for that box of Toolcards you make up to help you solve problems. |
| PST Toolcard | Those cards you create up to help you recall your tools for solving problems. (Appendix A) |
| Question Bag | A mental metaphor for our set of all questioning tools and skills. |

| | |
|---|---|
| Rule Of Life | Those bits of wisdom or silliness that we collect along the way if we keep our eyes, ears, etc. open as we drive along. Many of these are inherently silly, others seem really wise. Most seem, if you keep any kind of eye on them at all, to switch from side to side, wise to foolish, until they often occupy both sides at once. ROL 21b: If you can keep track, or at least tolerate, that concept of reality you have achieved a high level of thinking, if not necessarily wisdom. (See future volume "How To Wisdom.") BTW: These rules don't truly have fixed numbers in my world. I just slap interesting looking/sounding numbers on when I invoke one to make it appear that it might be that way to the casual reader. |
| Same but Different | The skill of comparing new ideas or problems with old or existing ones. Seeing the familiar inside the new. |
| See with New Eyes | Looking at a problem, solution, or anything as if you had never seen it before. Innocent. |
| Suspend Belief or Disbelief | The ability to open your mind to new or to familiar situations or ideas regardless of your existing ideas or world view. |
| Sideways Thinking | See Lateral Thinking. |
| Wait-and-See | A decision to observe the problem or situation further to see what develops. Often used with little or no action it can also be applied to any level of implementation of a problem solution. |
| Why/why Not | The skill of questioning from both or multiple sides of an idea. Willingness to consider other angles or conflicting ideas. |

## Further Resources for students & teachers:

## Books:

Curtis, Charles P. & Greenslet, Ferris, Ed., *The Practical Cogitator: The Thinker's Anthology, 3rd Edition*, 1962. == Collected essays on a wide range of topics. A good book to dip into over time.

Doering, Hod, *Squish Art, An Imagination Tool, Second Edition*, The Poetry Barn, 2000. == Fun creativity enhancement exercise.

Duncan, Ronald Frederick Henry, & Smith, Miranda W., *Encyclopedia of Ignorance*, Simon & Schuster Adult Publishing Group, March 1979. == Provides an interestingly different look at scientific thinking. Out of print – available used.

Hofstadter, Douglas R., *Gödel, Escher, Bach: An Eternal Golden Braid*, HarperCollins, 1999. == Not for the weak of heart. It won a 1979 Pulitzer and has been reprinted. Some few of the predictions are now outdated. I recall the experience of reading this one with fondness. One of the most challenging books I ever read, but worth the work. My head got bigger as I read.

Sloane, Paul & MacHale, Des, *Improve Your Lateral Thinking: Puzzles To Challenge Your Mind*, Sterling Publishing, 1995. == There are a series of these lateral thinking exercise books by Sloane with various coauthors. I have six or so of these. Good for class use as well.

Thorpe, Scott, *How to Think Like Einstein: Simple Ways to Break the Rules and Discover Your Hidden Genius*, Sourcebooks Trade, 2000. == Many good ideas.

Twain, Mark, *Pudd'nhead Wilson*, Reissue, Signet Classics, 1976. Classic short novel. Interesting, worth it for the Calendar chapter headings.

von Oech, Roger, *A WHACK ON THE SIDE OF THE HEAD : How You Can Be More Creative*, Warner Business; Revised edition, December 1, 1998 == there is also card deck to go along with this book. A good starter.

Busch, Heather & Silver, Burton, *Why Cats paint*, Ten Speed Press, 1994

Websites:

http://www.merriam-webster.com == Good dictionary site.

http://www.austhink.org/critical/about.htm

http://www.criticalthinking.org == good jumpoff site as well as having thoughtful resources of its own.

http://www.creativequotations.com/ == Look up your favorite quote. Use random quotes to inspire yourself.

http://home.freeuk.net/elloughton13/ == Creative, a nice offering from an elementary school.

http://www.thinking-allowed.com/ == Hosted by Jeffrey Mishlove, Ph.D., Thinking Allowed is a long-running independent public television series and has an extensive video library developed from the series. Thinking Allowed aims to provide an open, non-adversarial forum for the exchange of intelligent, alternative ideas.

http://www.kcmetro.cc.mo.us/longview/ctac/toc.htm == resources compiled by Longview Community College in Missouri.

www.everypoet.com/archive/poetry/Joyce_Kilmer/Joyce_Kilmer_trees_trees.htm == read the entire Kilmer poem. There are many more in the everypoet archives as well.

http://archivesofamericanart.si.edu/exhibits/sketchbk/sketchbk.htm == Titled Visual Thinking interesting sketching from professional artists.

http://www.grandin.com/inc/visual.thinking.html == Autistic PhD gives insight into alternate manner of thinking. Interesting for those who wish to expand their thinking world.

http://www.rit.org/ == Includes many basic skill essays as well as some more advanced.

## Probably more useful for teachers:

Finke, R.A., Ward, T.B. & Smith, S.M., *Creative Cognition*, Bradford/MIT Press, 1992.

Marks-Tarlow, T., *Creativity inside out: Learning through multiple intelligences*, Addison-Wesley, 1995.

Sternberg, R.J., *The Nature of Creativity*, Cambridge University Press, 1988.

VanGundy, A.B. *Creative Problem Solving*, Quorum, 1987.

http://www.library.ucsb.edu/untangle/jones.html == rather scholarly resource.

For many more thinking references type "think", "creative thinking", "thinking like", "thinker", or similar phrases into your favorite search engine; try http://www.google.com if you don't have a favorite.

# Index

**#**

3000 Times Rule, 14

**A**

Analyze The Problem, 29
Art Of Thinking, 57
Autopilot, 42

**B**

Brainstorming Ground Rules, 34
Brainstorming Steps, 36
Brainstorming, 33
Breaking The Rules, 33
Bustling Backwater, 2

**C**

Cheating, 20
Combined Solution, 22
Conceptual Blocks, 50
Conscious Comprehension, 14
Conscious Thinking, 14
Consider All Viewpoints, 35
Corollary, 14
Crazy Person, 53
Crazy Thinking, 53
Create The Solution, 29
Creating Smaller Problems, 25
Creative Thinking, 9
Critical Thinker, 57
Critical Thinking, 9

**D**

Deductive Reasoning, 65
Develop The Solution, 29
Discuss And Combine, 37

**E**

Editor, 42
Everyone Contributes, 36
Everything I Know Is Wrong, 51
Exercise, 13

**F**

Filters, 42
Formal Problem Solving, 28
Formal Statement Of The Problem, 28
Free Exchange Of Ideas, 34
Fuzzy Logic, 68

**G**

Get Practical, 37
Great Thinkers, 60

**H**

Human Learning Rule, 14
Hypothesis, 23

**I**

If It Works Don't Fix It, 49
Implement The Solution, 15
Inductive Reasoning, 31
Inspiration, 40

**M**

Mixed Problem, 22

## N

Never Completely Discard Ideas, 36
New Problem, 31
Next Case, 65
Non-Solution, 37

## O

Old Problem, 17
One-Three Punch, 22

## P

Pedagogy, 75
PPP, 3
Problem Solving Thinking, 1, 71
Problem, 13
PST General Rule 1, 21
PST General Rule 2, 24
PST General Rule 3, 25
PST General Rule 4, 26
PST General Rule 5, 28
PST General Rule 6, 33
PST Toolbox, 2
PST Toolcard, 71
PST, 2
Pun, 9

## Q

Question Bag, 18

## R

Regular Thinking, 25
Review And Revise, 30
Road Sign, 3
Roadside Attraction, 3
Rules Are Bad, 48

## S

Same And/But Different, 26
Scenic Overlook, 2
See With New Eyes, 22
Side Trip, 2
Sideways Or Lateral Thinking, 53
SIP, Simple Idea Possibility, 46
Super-Tweaking, 15
Suspend Disbelief And Belief, 47
SWIG, Sophisticated Wild Idea Guess, 46
System Tweaking, 30

## T

The Scientific Method, 23
Thinking Toolbox, 2, 71
Thinking Tools, 10
Thought Experiment, 23
Too Big Problem, 25

## U

Unconscious Comprehension, 14

## W

Wait-And-See, 37
Why or Why Not, 52
Words You Need To Know, 2

## Z

Zone Of Incomprehension, 14
Zone Of Conscious Comprehension, 14
Zone Of Unconscious Comprehension , 14